Evaluating a Performance

M000033079

Michael Greenwald
Texas A&M University

New York Boston San Francisco
London Toronto Sydney Tokyo Singapore Madrid
Mexico City Munich Paris Cape Town Hong Kong Montreal

i

Evaluating a Performance, by Michael Greenwald

ISBN: 0-321-09541-3

4 5 6 7 8 9 10 - CRW - 04 03 02

CONTENTS

Appendixes

ACT ONE:
PREPARING FOR YOUR ROLE AS AUDIENCE AND CRITIC

The Overture:[1]

Why Should I Write a Review?

Writing a review of a play-in-performance offers a chance for you—as a member of an audience and an indispensable participant in the theater event—to participate actively in the process of creating theater. Sure, you can do this without writing a review, and in most cases you should go to the theater simply to enjoy the work of the artists, to reflect on the play and its ideas, and to discuss your experience with friends after the show.

However, writing about the theater is an invaluable way to enhance your experience because:

- it allows you to apply what you have learned about the theater to a specific play;
- it encourages you to consider what you have experienced and transform it into ideas of your own;
- it enhances your critical thinking and writing skills (resources you will use in virtually any career you choose; this is a life skills exercise!).

So don't think of writing a review as a burden. It's an interesting opportunity for you to play a role—that of the critic, one of the most challenging and rewarding jobs in the theater.

You need not have written a play or acted, directed, or designed a set to be a thoughtful critic. Your requirements? An idea sparked by a play or performance and the means to articulate that idea clearly and vividly. And remember, criticism is an "act" we each perform daily as we judge the food we eat, the music we listen to, the lectures we hear, and the TV shows we watch. Most of our criticism is simple: "I liked it," "It was awesome," "It was boring," or "I hated it." When dealing with things

---

[1] An *overture* is a musical selection played before a production that puts the audience in the proper mood to enjoy the play. It is also an invitation to join, to take part in.

prepared to do some critical writing, especially now that you have some knowledge about theater and drama.

If you are not doing so already, make it part of your continuing theater education to read reviews regularly. Not only will it keep you abreast of what's new in the theater, it will enable you to sharpen your critical thinking skills by learning from professionals. Newspapers in major cities, magazines such as *Time, Newsweek* and *Rolling Stone,* and theater journals such as *American Theatre* regularly contain reviews. Soon you will find critics whose style and opinions you value. Also, each year since 1940 virtually every review of plays performed in New York has been collected and bound under the title of *New York Theatre Critics' Reviews* (now *The National Theater Critics' Reviews*); this series should be in your campus library. By no means should you take everything you read at face value. Learn to be as discriminating in your reading of reviews as you are in your theater going. It will not take you long to distinguish quality critical writing from inferior work, even if you have not seen the play in question.

Choices: Thinking Along with the Artists

When theater artists talk to each other, they often use phrases such as "I like your choices there." Stage directors exhort actors to "make bold choices, " a costume designer researches fashion history to choose the right silhouette for a show, and a lighting designer sorts through sheets of gels (colored light filters) to select the right hue for a scene. Thus, *choice* is a crucial term for theater artists—and critics—just as plays are about human choices and their consequences

Clear, innovative choices can heighten the theater experience, while predictable or ill-conceived ones can produce a long evening for everyone. Writing theater criticism can be a richer experience if you think along with the artists who produce the play. As you write your review, you are ultimately assessing the choices made by the playwright, the actors and their director, and the design and technical artists. So, think like an artist. Ask yourself:

- Why was this choice made?
- Was it the most effective choice possible? Why? Or why not?

- What are some alternative choices that may have been more successful?

Incidentally, as you write your review, you, too, will be making choices: what to talk about; which words to use; how to structure your thoughts most effectively. When your instructor reads your review, she or he will be assessing the quality of your choices in the review (just as you will assess his or her choice of a grade!). See—criticism, you can't escape it.

This workbook is designed to lead you through the process of writing a play review. We've even structured your task as a play. In act One, we'll start with the first choice you must make: *What play should I see* (assuming you have an option)? Then we'll go step-by-step through the process of getting to your seat and preparing to see the play. This is all exposition for Act Two: assessing the play and its performance as you watch it. In Act Three you'll actually write the review and, as your curtain call, even evaluate the completed review. So, on with the show!

Scene 1:
Your Role in the Theater Event

Why You Are as Important as the Actors

There are four indispensable elements in the theater event:

- An idea to be communicated (usually in a script);
- Performers to communicate the idea;
- A space in which the idea is performed (and it doesn't have to be a formal theater);
- An audience (even of one) to receive the idea.

And that's why you are as important as the actors: theater cannot exist without an audience. Rehearsals can—but not a bona fide theater event.

And just as laughing, booing, applauding, crying are means through which the audience's can "talk back" to the performers, so too does writing a review helps you complete the communication process. The

3

performer may not read your review, but you are still talking back to the production.

What's Playing?

If your instructor has assigned a play to you, you'll find that there are several advantages to the assigned play:

- If it is a play you have read and discussed in class, you will be especially well-prepared to talk about the play with confidence;
- If your class is seeing the same production, it allows you to compare your perceptions against those of your peers (but remember: art is subjective by its nature, and there is no single valid critical response to a production);
- You don't have to worry about finding a play, the theater, or perhaps even getting tickets.

Finding a play on your own is not difficult—usually—and it can be an enlightening experience itself because it will acquaint you with the many types of plays produced in your area. Also, you can probably find a play that suits your interests and degree of sophistication. If this will be your first visit to a professional theater, by all means choose something that will most likely provide a positive experience.

There are several reliable sources that will help you find the right play for you:

- *Newspapers*: Both daily newspapers and some weekly publications (often found 'free' in book and music stores or coffee bars) list plays being performed in the area. Most major newspapers now publish an entertainment guide (usually on Thursday and/or Sunday) that not only lists productions, but often provide a capsule review of the play. Especially good productions are often flagged with four or five stars or a notation like "Critics' Choice," which usually indicates quality work.

- If you're going to be in New York and want to see a Broadway play, most major newspapers usually run something called a "Broadway Box Score" in the Sunday arts section. Here you'll not only get a list of Broadway (and some off-Broadway) plays,

4

but an indicator of how difficult it is to get tickets to popular shows like *The Lion King*.

- *The 'Net*: Most cities of size now have a web page that has an "Arts and Entertainment" page. Here you'll find a list of plays, names and addresses of theaters, etc. Most theaters have their own web page; you can click on to a theater's web page and get all the information you need (often including play summaries and reviews). And in most cases, you can even order tickets on line.

- Theater managers will tell you that the best advertising for a play is still word-of-mouth. Ask around—someone you know has probably seen a good show, or heard about one.

Getting Tickets

Now that your professor has assigned a play, or you've found a show that interests you, it is time to buy tickets. There are several ways to go about buying tickets:

- The theater's own *box office* is the most obvious source. You can often get better seating directly from the box office (and can often view a seating chart); and if you go directly to the box office you can usually save the grotesque service charges ticket agencies charge (and even some theaters tack on a service charge for phone reservations). Of course you have to go to the theater itself, which means gas and parking expenses.

- Many cities, especially New York and London, have *ticket agencies* that will sell you very good seats at a hefty markup. But if it's the only way you can see a hot show, it may be worth the extra money. Ticketron and other phone and/or internet services make ticket shopping easy from your home, but they do charge for their services (ask Pearl Jam!).

- If you are a 'starving student' there some excellent ways of going to the theater 'on the cheap:'

5

- *Student Rush*: Many theaters have a "student rush" policy that allows students (with ID) to purchase any unsold seats at hugely discounted prices, usually one half hour before the performance. You've got to be patient and a bit of a gambler to get rush seats, but it can save you a bundle. Call the theater and ask about rush seats; if they are available, go to the theater at least an hour before the performance and get in the rush line. Sometimes you can get very lucky and a patron with a ticket or two to sell—or give away!—will negotiate a deal with you.
- *TKTS Booths*: Following New York's lead (and now London), many cities with multiple theaters have a centrally located ticket booth where you can purchase "day of" tickets at half-price (plus a small service charge). Theaters send over unsold tickets for that day, and people who don't mind lines can buy these tickets cheaply. In New York this agency is called TKTS, and you can find similar operations in such cities as Minneapolis, San Diego, and Denver. Again, check a city's web page for information about such outlets.
- *Group sales*: Many theaters sell generously discounted tickets to groups of 10 or more. This is especially true of not-for-profit theaters that receive grant money by agreeing to make tickets available to student groups at substantial discounts. For instance, Houston's Alley Theater sells $30+ seats for $11.50 to student groups of 10 or more. Organize a group of friends and classmates for a theater trip. Contact the group sales manager at the theater.
- *Ads*: Check the personals ads in the newspaper: there is usually a section devoted to tickets (usually rock concerts and ball games) where you can often find theater tickets for sale.
- *Ushering*: You can volunteer to usher for a show; in exchange for a couple of hours work, you can escort people to their seats to receive some leftover seats or standing room tickets. (Senior citizens see many free shows doing this.) Call the theater and ask about its ushering policies. You may be able to see an entire season's worth of plays (worth hundreds of dollars) as a volunteer usher.

Scene 2
Preparing for Your Role as a Critic

To what degree should you prepare yourself to see a play in performance? Should you read the play, about the play, about the playwright, and about the production before you see it? Or should you merely show up like most of the audience, sit back, enjoy the show, and then write about your experience? There are advantages to each:

- *Preparing* (in most cases) allows you to get the most out of your experience:
  - o you know the play and have some ideas about its meaning;
  - o you can match your interpretation against that of the actors and director;
  - o you can concentrate on the performances and designs rather than the plot and characters.

- *Not preparing* allows you to
  - o come to the play like most audiences (both now and when the play was originally performed);
  - o provide a "gut" response to the play and its production, which can be the most honest reaction.

Your instructor may expect you to prepare before seeing a play (as most professional critics do). All things considered, it is probably a good idea to familiarize yourself before seeing the play; chances are, your final review will be that much stronger. So let's assume you need to lay some groundwork before seeing the production.

Reading (and Watching) the Play

You have probably learned something about play analysis from your instructor and your textbook, so there's no need to tread old ground here. As you read and watch the play, however, you might ask yourself some questions about the principal dramatic, theatrical, and aesthetic elements inherent in the script. Of course, you cannot address all of these questions in a review, but your answers will help shape your written assessment of the play and its production. In many cases, what may seem to be a weakness in the play as you read it may be diminished in a good production; good actors, directors, and designers can often make a script appear stronger than it is (and, of course, the reverse is also true at times).

■ NOTE: There is an *Evaluating a Performance Worksheet* in the appendix to this book (see page 49). You may want to complete it as you read the play and then revise it after you've seen the production. Also, consult the *glossary* in your theater textbook in case you are not familiar with some of these terms. ■

Some questions to keep in mind as you read or watch the play:

Genre:
- What is the genre—i.e., literary classification—of the play?
  - o Serious Drama
    - ▪ Tragedy
    - ▪ Drama
    - ▪ Melodrama
  - o Comic Drama
    - ▪ Comedy of Manners
    - ▪ Satire
    - ▪ Farce
    - ▪ Slapstick
  - o Tragicomedy
  - o History
  - o Musical
    - ▪ Musical Comedy
    - ▪ Dramatic Musical
    - ▪ Opera
    - ▪ Operetta

Plotting, structure, action:
- What kind of plot has the playwright used? (See the worksheet "Evaluating a Performance" on page 49 of this book as well as the terminology guide that accompanies it.)
  The climactic plot
  The episodic (epic) plot:
  The cyclic plot:
  The "plotless" play
- Is there a discernable storyline that engages the audience?
- If there is a subplot, how does it contribute to the play's tension and meaning?

- Does the story unfold in such a way to intensify audience involvement?
- Are there well-defined conflicts between characters and ideologies?
- Is there sufficient dramatic tension to hold the audience's attention?
- Is the action developed credibly--i.e., do events seem to grow naturally and plausibly out of one another?
- Is the crisis logically resolved? If the playwright chooses not to resolve the principal crisis, is there a thematic reason?

Characters:
- Are the characters interesting and engaging?
- Are any of the characters "archetypes"—i.e., universal symbols of human behavior? Can you relate them to other archetypes?
- What do the characters want and what are they doing to get it?
- Which characters are primary? Secondary? Background?
- Are all the characters necessary?
- Who is the protagonist and what major change does he or she undergo during the course of the play? If there is not a discernable change, why?
- Who is the antagonist and why is he or she in conflict with the protagonist? What means does he or she use to thwart the will of the antagonist?
- Are the principal characters sufficiently developed and dynamic? If they are static, is there sufficient dramatic reason for their inertia?
- Do we learn more about the characters from their actions or from the dialogue?
- Are the characters consistent within your understanding of human nature?
- Is there a compelling reason why we should know these characters?

Language:
- Is the language interesting and memorable, yet appropriate to the play? Its characters? The situation?
- Is the play written in:
  o Prose

- o Poetry
- o A combination of Prose and Poetry?
- Why has the playwright selected this particular mode of communication?
- Is there variety in the language? Is there sufficient distinction among the characters' language within the play?
- What is the overall quality of the writing? Is it fresh and inventive? Or trite and predictable? Cite instances of an especially well-written speech or line.
- Is there a balance between realistic and theatrical dialogue?
- Is there a justification for the theatrical language?

Themes and Ideas:
- What are the central ideas of the play? Are they treated freshly and with new insight?
- Does the playwright "preach" or does the action and character interaction convey the play's ideas?
- Is there a balance between thought and emotion?
- Are opposing viewpoints given sufficient weight in the argument?
- Are the characters that promote the ideas credible?
- Is there a speech, or even a line, that represents the playwright's thematic concerns?

The World of the Play:
- Does the playwright create an interesting world into which the audience wants to enter?
- Are the playwright's use of writing and playing conventions appropriate?
- At what level of realism does the playwright want the play to work?
- How might you classify the "style" of this play? Some styles include:
  - o Realism, Naturalism
  - o Theatrical
  - o Classical
  - o Romantic
  - o Absurdist
  - o Expressionism, Surrealism
  - o Post-modern

(*Reminder*: A production may impose a different style on a play than that for which it was written.)

Emotions:
- Does the play sufficiently engage the audience's emotions?
- Is there sufficient emotional variety within the play?
- Do the emotions overwhelm the play, its action, and its language? Is there a balance between thought and emotions?
- Do the characters tell us their feelings or do their actions show them?
- Where is the emotional climax to the play?

Aesthetics:
- Does the play have universal appeal?
- Does the playwright give us insight into the chaos of daily life and strengthen our own means of facing it?
- Does the play provide a satisfactory experience for the audience?

Theatrical Elements:

(*Reminder*: A director may add musical and theatrical elements that are not scripted; he or she may also "cut" some that are scripted)

- Is *music* integral to the play? Does it advance the action? Create mood? What are the degrees of realism and/or artificiality in the play?
- Is the play written to be played in one of two styles:
  o *Presentational* (i.e., it acknowledges the presence of the audience and often directs speeches to the audience) or
  o *Representational* (i.e., it pretends to be a "slice of life" and does not acknowledge the presence of the audience)?
- To what degree is *spectacle* important to this play?
- Are there inherently theatrical elements and conventions in the script?
  o Masks, "costumes" (other than regular clothing)
  o Unusual scenery or props
  o Tableaux, freezes
  o Non-realistic lighting and sound effects

11

Reading About the Play

Not only is it useful to read the play before seeing it, it may be as useful to read *about* it as well. This can be done in several ways:

- *Reviews of the play*: You may have a chance to read a review of the play by the local theater critic in the newspaper. The danger, of course, is that it may unduly influence your opinion of the play and/or its production. On the other hand, you may feel quite differently than the critic and can argue your case in your review (and it is fair game to take issue with a published review). Also, you can read reviews of the play when it was first performed in a variety of sources, most notably in an annual collection of reviews called *The National Theater Critics' Reviews*. You can also find reviews of plays on the internet.
  (*Reminder*: Your instructor is familiar with these sources, too: don't try to pass off a review you've lifted from the 'Net. Most instructors can quickly tell the difference between student and professional writing.)

- *Essays about a play*: Textbooks, critical studies, journals and even the 'Net have detailed essays about well-known plays. Reading a couple of these may help focus your thinking about the play before you see it.

- *Interviews and pre-show newspaper stories*: You can often find interesting, informative "pre-show" stories about a play in local papers. Usually within a week of its opening, a theater critic will sometimes interview the playwright if possible, (especially for new plays), the director and some actors for a feature story meant to induce audiences to attend the play. Here you may find some useful insights about the production from the artists themselves.

- *"Informances:"* Many regional theaters now include a pre-show introduction to the play, usually led by the theater's dramaturg (a literary expert who advises the director). Also, many theaters offer "talk backs," which artists and audience members discuss the production after the curtain call. Both can give you insights into the artistic choices that shaped the production. These events don't happen every night, so check with the theater to see if they have "informances" or "talk backs."

New Plays

In the case of new plays, especially premieres (first productions) there may not be as many pre-show resources available to you. Scripts may not have been published, and certainly there will not be reviews, essays, and other background material. You should, however, be able to find feature stories about the production in the newspaper; these almost always have interviews with the playwright and often the director. Much of this pre-show information and press clippings are available on the theater's web page or in the lobby of the theater. Take the time to look at the press clippings before you enter the theater.

Leaving for the Theater

The final steps in the preparation stage are easy, although you may have some legitimate questions about:

- *What do I wear?* It used to be that people dressed formally when going to the theater, but today that is pretty much limited to "first nighters" and special events. Today you can go to the theater dressed comfortably and casually and no one will object. However, for some people "dressing up" is part of the enjoyment of going to the theater, especially larger theaters, at night, and during the fall, winter, and early spring. Summer theater is invariably casual, especially if it is held outdoors.

- *How early should I arrive at the theater?* Many theaters have a strict policy that "latecomers will be seated at the discretion of the management." Those who are late are often held in the lobby, where they may be able to watch the first scene (or act) on TV monitors. Latecomers are a huge distraction in the theater (more so than in movie houses) because they are usually lit. Actors absolutely hate latecomers and have been known to berate those who arrive after the play has begun (Katherine Hepburn was notorious for this!). Allow plenty of time to get to the theater, get parked, and into the lobby. Many theaters provide pre-show entertainment (e.g., a piano player in the lobby) and there are usually interesting displays (often of design renderings and models) to look at. It's best to be in the lobby at least a half-hour before the curtain.

Scene 3
Making Your Entrance

Unlike movie theaters—where you enter, stop by the concession stand, and enter a darkened auditorium to watch advertisements on the screen before the film begins—there is a bit more to live theater. The various pre-show elements help make the theater event 'special' and even a bit ritualistic. More practically, your impressions of the production are often colored by your experience from the moment you enter the theater. If this is your first trip to a professional theater, you may want to familiarize yourself with some of the people and things you'll encounter.

Front of House

In addition to the ticket takers (who tend to be quite friendly and who will indicate the general direction of your seats), you'll usually see a well-dressed person (with a two-way radio) who supervises all activity in the lobby. This is the *house manager*, a kind of maitre d' who tries to keeps things moving so the show starts on time. The house manager also wants to keep patrons happy, so if you run into a problem that an usher cannot handle, ask to speak to the house manager.

Do take a few minutes to look at any lobby displays before going to your seats. Design displays, set models, costume pieces, cast photos, and the like are intended to get you in the proper mindset to watch the play. Sometimes it can be part of the fun to compare an actor's "head shot" (an 8x10 glossy photo) with what you actually see on stage.

When you get to the section where your seats are located, you will be greeted by an usher who will usually escort you to the aisle in which you will sit; ushers also tell you exactly which seats are yours. If in doubt: check! It's disruptive and embarrassing to have to move to other seats. Your usher will also give you a program (more on programs below).

Theater Etiquette

Before you settle into your seat, it's best to remove coats (large coats, backpacks, etc., may be checked in the lobby). Be sure to turn off cell phones and beepers; it goes without saying that they are an enormous distraction in live theater. Frankly, if you are expecting an "emergency call," you probably shouldn't be at the theater in the first place.

Sir Tyrone Guthrie, the much-admired stage director, once said that in the theater "a cough is a criticism." When audiences get restless, coughing is usually one of the first signs that a show is in trouble (and you may want to note this as you judge the production). Many theaters provide cough drops and throat lozenges for those with legitimate health problems. If you're a cougher, pick up some on the way into the theater (or bring them with you).

Unfortunately, in our TV age audiences are used to talking while watching TV and movies. While this is inexcusable in most situations, it is especially distracting in the theater. You will not only disrupt others who are trying to hear the dialogue, actors are sensitive to unwanted interference and it can affect the quality of their work. By all means, laugh, clap or cry if you are so moved, but don't talk while the actors are working. And candy wrappers and munching food are also notorious distractions; most theaters do not allow food or drink in the auditorium.

Also, while we usually think nothing of people walking out of a movie to get some popcorn or use the bathroom, it is considered very rude behavior in the live theater. Again, it disrupts the actors, and, in some cases, it may even be dangerous if actors must enter through the audience.

Should I take notes during the production?
Professional critics are very good at scribbling notes unobtrusively in the dark. If you must take notes, do so as carefully and as quietly as you can. Usually a key word or two will suffice. It's best to scribble notes between scenes or at intermission and shortly after the play. Actors do not like to perform to an audience of note takers. And they really, really hate penlights!

Looking Around

Even as you are settling into your seat, you will automatically begin assessing the production. Among the things you should consider include:

What type of theater am I in?
- *Proscenium*: this is the "picture frame" stage that usually separates the performers from the audience; it is especially conducive to spectacular scenery.
- *Thrust*: the audience usually sits on three sides of the stage; this promotes stronger interaction between actors and audience, yet still allows for scenery.
- *Arena*, or theater-in-the-round: the audience surrounds the stage on all sides and is, therefore, usually close to the action; scenery is usually kept to a minimum.
- *Transverse*: the audience sits on two side of the stage.
- *Environmental*: for some experimental productions, the artists create a particular stage configuration that is specific to that play; often the audience is asked to move around.
- *Open air*: any of the above may be used in outdoor settings, especially for summer performances; but with open air theater there may be other distractions (traffic, unwanted lighting, other buildings, spectacular scenery, etc.).

What do I see on the stage before the show?
- If the curtain is down, you won't see much. A lowered curtain, however, can create a sense of anticipation. Frankly, the lowered curtain is not used much anymore because directors and designers now like to create a mood before the show. If the curtain is lowered, it is actually something of an oddity and may arouse your interest as you wonder what is hidden behind the curtain.
- Typically, you will be able to see the setting, although it will be dimly lit. Often the set will be lit with a "pre-show wash," a colorful pattern of lights meant to create mood. Do take some time to look carefully at the set and gather hints about the play-to-come. This will be your first chance to look at— and assess—the first choices offered by the director and

16

designers. The communication process has begun and you should ask yourself what is being communicated.

Can lighting instruments be seen? What is the lighting communicating?
- If the lighting instruments are obvious and there has been little attempt to hide them, it is usually an indication that the show will be more theatrical than realistic. The more blatant the lighting instruments are shown—especially if they are using non-naturalistic colors—the more theatrical the production is intended to be.
- The color and patterning of the lights help create mood and atmosphere. Take a moment to assess how the lighting makes you 'feel' as you look at it. What kinds of expectations does the lighting create? The director and lighting designer are already working on your feelings.

Is there pre-show music? What mood does it create? What does it suggest about the impending production?
- Directors and sound designers often spend hours finding exactly the right mood music for a play, so it is often a good indicator of things to come.
- Does the music create a specific emotion? Or is it used to establish time and place? Or a bit of both? Consider the music you hear (if any) and ask why the director chose that particular music.
- Is the music too loud, too distracting? Pre-show music should not inhibit the audience; it should work more subliminally.

Are there pre-show diversions?
- Occasionally you may find actors on stage or among the audience before the show. They are most likely trying to establish time, place, mood, and other things that will help the audience enter the world of the play. Such "pre-shows" are always calculated for their effect, so ask yourself why the director has made such an obvious choice.
- Pre-shows should usually be subtle and not compete for attention with the actual show. A good pre-show is one which you watch for a minute or two, then return to your program, your friends, and so on.

Once you've absorbed the theater space, the settings, the music, and perhaps a pre-show, you should take a few moments to peruse the program (another good reason to arrive early!). You'll find information that will help you enjoy the play—and write your review.

The *cover* (which may be a reproduction of the production's poster) often tells you something about the play. Good cover and poster designs try to crystallize the mood and even the idea of the play in a single, fetching image. Ask yourself:

- What do the cover/poster design, the lettering, the layout suggest?
- How does it make me feel?
- Does it seem to symbolize an idea?
- What expectations about the play and the production does it arouse in me?

There is usually a *"title page"* for the play, where you will find the names of the playwright, producer(s), director, designers, and key support staff (e.g., dance and stage combat choreographers). You'll need their names when writing the review, so note them now.

A *"cast of characters"* (or *dramatis personae*—"people in the drama") page is usually next. Here you find the characters and the actors who play them. Often there will be a brief character description ("an elderly widow") or relationship ("George's brother") to help you keep the characters straight. You might note that some roles are "doubled" or even "tripled:" an actor will play more than one role.

If you see an actor named "George Spelvin," by the way, it usually is a stage name for an actor playing a small role in addition to a larger one (or more). Actors frequently list their walk-ons as 'George Spelvin'—it's an old theater tradition and a nice "in joke" for those who know.

Also, on the "characters" page, there is usually an indicator of *time and place*. This can be especially useful to denote time lapses between scenes. And many theaters indicate how many *intermissions* (or *intervals*) you may expect, and the duration of each. If there is no intermission, you will be told that, too. More and more theaters are now indicating the *running time* of the production. Do take the time to note all of these before the play begins.

In the program you may also find a note from the director explaining his or her concept for the play. There may also be some useful background information about the play, the playwright, or even the period in which the play is set. A production of *Julius Caesar*, for instance, might have some historical information that will increase your understanding of the play. A stage history of the play, especially if it is a classic, may also be found in the program.

If you are seeing a musical, you will usually find a list of songs and the order in which they appear. The character that sings the song is usually noted as well. You'll want this information as you write the review. You may find it useful to review this page when you get home: you'll be surprised by the vivid memories you'll have of the production by looking at the cast of characters and musical numbers pages.

Do take time to read the cast and crew bios if they are in the program. You may be impressed by the vast training and experience the actors possess, and you may not have to spend the production wondering "where have I seen that face before?" if you know that the actor played on a soap opera five years ago! Mostly, it is a courtesy to the actors and other artists to survey their work.

Finally, the program will have information about the theater (where are the bathrooms?), upcoming plays, how to get season tickets, and so on. And there are often coupons for post-show drinks and food at nearby restaurants.

A final note about programs: it's probably best to keep your program open to the cast of characters page so you don't have to fumble for the page during the performance. Rustling programs, like coughs, are another indicator that a show is losing its audience. As Hamlet said to the Players, "*use all gently*" while watching a play. The actors and those around you will appreciate it.

NOTES

ACT TWO:
ON WITH THE SHOW:
EVALUATING THE PERFORMANCE

From the moment you entered the theater you have been—both consciously and subconsciously—forming opinions about your experience. You may have admired a beautiful lobby and a grand staircase leading into the theater; you may have found the auditorium inviting or cold and formidable. You no doubt have studied the set and the pre-show lighting if there was no curtain. If the show began twenty minutes late, you may already be restless and unimpressed with the theater (that's why people need to be on time!). So your critical skills are already at work.

Still, there is something of a fresh start when the lights fade to black, the audience grows quiet, and the curtain raises or the lights come up. Over the next two hours or so, you will constantly (if not always knowingly) be making critical assessments of what you see and hear. There are numerous things about which you could write in your review, and no single review can cover them all. In this "act," we'll consider the individual components of a performance, provide some questions you might ask yourself as you encounter each, and alert you to some things you might not otherwise think about.

Scene 1:
First and Final Impressions

You may recall that in almost every case theater throughout the world began as a ritual, most often in conjunction with religious or agricultural events (or both). Although the modern theater is primarily a commercial and diversionary experience, there remains a sense of ritual in the structure of a play and in its performance. Accordingly, the opening sequence of a production and its final moments are especially important. Each contributes much to your appreciation of the play, and each provides the production with a formal "sense of occasion."

Raising the Curtain and Your Expectations

Someone once said that a speaker has the audience's full attention and support for the first thirty seconds of the speech, and that the speaker can win or lose the audience in that short time. The same holds true for the theater, although the 'trial period' lasts a bit longer.

As the curtain rises, or the lights come on to illuminate the stage, there is usually an extraordinary energy throughout the theater. It truly is the beginning of a journey that the actors and audience will complete together, and it is for this reason that that opening sequence must set the tone for things to come. This doesn't mean there has to be a high-energy start; in fact, a more measured opening can be more effective as it allows the audience to take in the many visual and other sensory stimuli. A film opens with a specific shot at which the audience must look, but in the theater the audience has many things to look at. And people are more inclined to look than listen at the outset of a play, so most directors will invent an opening sequence that allows the audience to take in the sets, the costumes, props, the lighting, and the actors themselves.

Musicals, by the way, traditionally have their own formal beginning: the *overture*. The house lights dim, a spotlight is aimed at the orchestra pit (which is, in most cases, tucked under the forestage), the conductor bows to the audience, turns to the orchestra, the theater grows very quiet, and the musicians play a lively "preview" of the show's songs. The overture not only allows the audience to familiarize itself with the music, it sets the mood for the musical play that follows. After the overture, the audience is treated to a second opening as described above.

During the opening sequence, you might ask yourself:

- What emotions am I asked to feel during the opening sequence? What things help determine the emotional atmosphere: Color? Lighting? Music? Movement? The shape and size of the setting? Others?
- How quickly do the lights come up? How much of the stage is lit? How do these initial lighting choices affect my emotional and intellectual response to the first stage picture?
- Where am I asked to look first? What is the focal point of the stage?
- Is there a sense of harmony and balance on stage? Or does anything seem out of place?
- If there is more than one actor/character on stage, which initially seems to be the most important? What determines this: Costuming? Position? Movement? Lighting?

- What expectations does the opening stage picture arouse in me?
- What is the energy level on stage: Placid? Frenetic? How does this energy level affect my expectations?

The Curtain Call

While the formality of the opening sequence has a latent sense of ritual about it, the *curtain call*—in which the actors receive the applause of the audience after the play has ended—is truly a ritual because it is the symbolic leave-taking. The actors cease to be the characters, the audience formally 'thanks" the actors for their work, and all depart. There is something obviously artificial in a curtain call, yet is in some ways the most "real" aspect of the theater event because all pretense is dropped and everyone involved in the production—actors and audience—acknowledges that they have been involved in a theatrical event.

The crispness and energy of the curtain call leaves you with a final impression about the quality of the production. A well-staged curtain call provides a formal and classy way to end the show. More importantly, it gives you, the critic, a barometer by which to judge the audience's collective judgment of the play. You can quickly tell the difference between polite, perfunctory applause and a genuine enthusiasm for a job well done. And you can tell which actors most affected the audience by the volume and intensity of the applause. A standing ovation is generally the highest accolade that an audience can offer a cast, though some audiences are notorious for being too generous (or stingy) with SO's (as actors call them). The true test is how quickly the majority of the audience comes to its feet (some patrons can actually be bullied into standing because they don't want to seem ungenerous).

Lately it has become increasingly popular for actors to applaud the audience (something that has been done in Asian theater for centuries), partly to show their appreciation for the audience's attention, largely to acknowledge that the audience has helped create the theater event.

During the curtain call, consider some of the following:

- How enthusiastic is the applause, and how quickly does it come from the audience?

- Are the actors energetic and professional throughout the curtain call?
- Do actors remain "in character" and, if so, why?

Scene 2:
What's Happening ?

The first actors were no doubt storytellers that enlivened their stories by imitating the characters in their mighty tales. "Telling the story" remains an integral part of the theater event, although changes in style have, to some degree, diminished the plotting of a play. Today character often reins supreme in a play, thanks largely to our fascination with psychology. And there are, as we suggested in the section on play analysis, "plotless" plays.

Although some modern playwrights avoid such conspicuous plotting, you are most likely to see a well-defined storyline in the majority of plays and musicals. Most plays have a discernable structure:

- *Exposition*: background information about the characters and the plays issues are presented;
- *The Point of Attack*: that moment when the major conflict of a play is initiated;
- *The Complication (or Rising Action):* a series of minor crises and climaxes that advance the story and provide the dramatic tension that keeps the audience interested in the play;
- *The Crisis (or Obligatory Scene) and Climax*: invariably occurs late in the play and marks the moment when the conflict—usually between the protagonist and the antagonist—comes to a head and is resolved;
- *The Denouement*: the final moments of a play in which the various strands of the plot are 'tied up,' destinies are settled and a sense of equilibrium returns.

If you read the play in preparation for your visit to the theater, you probably noticed many of these plot elements, though some may have escaped you. In the performance, the director, through the actors and the designers, can heighten these plot elements with the aid of vocal coloring, movement and gestures, staging, focus, lighting, music, pauses or silences. Most importantly, the tension and the pace of the play (how quickly or leisurely it moves along) are usually the best indicators of good storytelling.

To assess how well the production tells the story, consider such questions as:

- Is the story line clear and comprehensible?
- Are key moments of exposition, crisis, climax, and resolution marked?
- Are these moments marked by theatrical means (lights, music, etc.)? By stage movement? By the actors' voices and/or intensity levels.
- Is the pacing consistent with the dramatic tension? Does the play drag? Does it move too quickly to be comprehensible?
- Were there moments when the audience, collectively, seemed to lose interest in the play? What were some of the signs of this restlessness? To what do you attribute this loss of interest?

NOTES:

Scene 3:
The Director

Although stage directors were, historically, among the last artists to enter the theater, they have become a potent force in the shaping of a production. For better or for worse, the theater of our day is sometimes referred to as "The Director's Theater," which implies that directors are often more important than actors. In theory, directors are meant to be the intermediaries between the playwright's script and the audience, but often they rival writers. Thoughtful directorial interpretation--which may border on invention--can be so illuminating that audiences feel as if they are seeing a new play and therefore append the director's name to the title. Or, at quite another extreme, directors can impose their vision on a script to the point where it is something other than what the playwright wrote. Thus, when evaluating the impact of a production, you are in many ways critiquing the work of the stage director.

The Director at Work

The theater director has four primary tasks:

1. Devising the Directorial Concept
2. Coordinating the Artists' Contributions
3. Creating an Aesthetic Experience
4. Helping the Actors

1. Devising the Directorial Concept

Long before the play is cast, the director studies the play. In some ways the director must know the play better than the playwright, a task which necessitates considerable research on the play, the playwright's style, the period in which it was written, the period in which it is set, the philosophical, historical, social, political and perhaps religious attitudes that shaped it, its production history, and the commentaries that critics and scholars offer on it. From this research—and perhaps some inspiration—the director devices a "concept:" that is, an interpretation of the play and the means used to express it.

The directorial concept usually works on two levels:
- *Internally*: the director looks for the play's "super-objective," or the central idea and emotional core that bind the play together.

- *Externally*: directors must consider the visual and aural elements that will best realize the concept; choosing a period in which to "dress" the play can be an important step towards realizing the directorial concept, particularly for classical plays.

The directorial concept narrows the field of choices for the performers and designers and thereby allows them to work more efficiently within given parameters. In an ideal world, of course, all of the artists involved in a production would contribute to the discovery of the concept, but the exigencies of "getting the show up" preclude this practice, especially in the commercial theater, where time is indeed money. Thus it is the director's task to define the objectives for the production.

2. Coordinating the Artists' Contributions

With so many artists and technicians contributing to a production, it is imperative that a central vision guides the work. Ideally the collaboration between the director and the designers and technicians, as well as the performers in the rehearsal hall, is somewhat democratic. Much of the director's non-rehearsal time is spent in conferences with designers and technicians at weekly production-team meetings and in one-on-one discussions. Such creative problem solving is as integral to the final product as what goes on in rehearsals.

3. Creating an Aesthetic Experience

Because an audience perceives a play imaginatively as well as intellectually and emotionally, directors attempt to make the theater experience memorable by the way in which they compose stage pictures and establish the rhythm and sound of the play. Directors need the eye of a master painter to group the actors on stage; indeed, a popular exercise for directing students is to look at the paintings of the masters to learn about groupings, body attitudes, and the like. There is, of course, the danger that blocking and stage composition can become mechanical and sterile. Directors provide visual variety by using different areas of the stage, height levels, linear and curved patterns, and other techniques to an aesthetically pleasing picture.

Directors also need to cultivate an orchestra conductor's sense of rhythm and tempo. Just as good musical piece changes tempos and volume, so too does a play and the director must guide not only the actors through the subtle variations, but also the technicians. If a play seems dull or static, it may not be entirely the actors' fault; perhaps the director has not provided a variety of visual and aural stimuli.

4. Helping the Actors

The director serves as an impartial observer who audits, evaluates, and adjusts the actors' work to develop truth and clarity. Early on in the production process, the director meets with actors for some "table talk," at which the individual characters are dissected. In rehearsal the director helps the actors make choices, always with an eye toward the whole. For example, a director may help actors break down difficult speeches or passages of verse. As the play takes shape and the individual actors bring their characters to life, the director helps them coalesce into an ensemble. As the actors advance beyond the exploratory stages, some directors tend to sit back and react to scenes. Many of the reactions are strictly technical: "I can't hear you there" or "You're speaking too quickly." Others address the psychological and emotional life of the character: "Why is he always so angry--aren't there other ways to react to a situation?" The director raises many of the same questions and criticisms that an audience member might. No wonder the fine British director Sir Tyrone Guthrie once called the director "the ideal audience of one."

Assessing the Director's Contributions

Although evaluating the quality of the director's work may be the most challenging aspect of writing a review because "the director's hand" is often less apparent than those of the actors and designers, you should consider some of the following as you think about the performance and complete the worksheet "Evaluating the Director" (on page 53 of this book):

Interpretation:
- Is there a logical, coherent interpretation of the play?
- Is the interpretation/concept supported by the script? If the director has chosen to play against the script, is there an internal logic to the alternative interpretation?
- Does the director seem to dominate the script?
- Do the directorial choices enhance your understanding of the play? Or do they compete with the script?

Visual Elements:
- Is there a central image or metaphor that helps define the play's dominant idea?
- Has the director created a plausible, interesting world for the play?
- Are there a variety of pleasing stage pictures?
- Are entrances and exits well motivated and choreographed, especially the "crowd scenes?"
- Are actors grouped so that proper focus is given to key characters?
- Are the performance, visual, aural, and technical elements coordinated to produce a unified effect?

Aesthetics:
- Does the play flow smoothly from one scene to the next?
- Does the production have effective rhythm and tempo?
- Is there sufficient variety in the pace of the play?
- Do the lighting effects, music, and other technical support enhance the experience of the play?
- Do the aesthetic elements call attention to themselves, or are they integrated into the whole?

Ensemble:
- Has the director created an ensemble among the actors?
- Are the acting styles compatible?
- Do the actors--individually and collectively--have a well-defined sense of the play's intellectual and emotional intentions?

NOTES

Scene 4:
The Actors

Whatever the contributions of the playwright and the director, ultimately any evaluation of a play must center upon the actors, not only because they are the most readily visible artists involved in a production, but because they are the first and least dispensable artists of the theater.

Put simply, an actor is "one who performs or impersonates." But "performs" and "impersonates" do not begin to define the reality of what the actor does. The award-winning actor Ellen Burstyn says, "Our work is much more dangerous than even that of an astronaut because we relive other people's pain."

We are "the most imitative of living creatures," declared Aristotle, which is to say that each of us brings a wealth of intuitive experience to the study of theater. Or as Marlon Brando put it: "Acting is something people think they are incapable of, but they do it from morning to night."

Approaches to Acting

Currently, there are three general approaches to the craft of acting:

1. The *external* approach, which relies primarily on voice and body to create the role, is largely a pre-twentieth century approach; this is most obvious in *stylized* (non-realistic) performances;
2. The *internal* approach, which relies primarily on personal experience (emotion memory) and psychology to create the role, is essentially a late-nineteenth/twentieth century approach and is most associated with *realistic* performances;
3. The *integrated* approach, which synthesizes the external and internal approaches.

Virtually all of pre-twentieth century drama necessitated an *external* approach to performance. Large theaters, scripts whose poetry and song demanded an enormous vocal range, conventions such as men or young boys playing women's roles, performing with few or no rehearsals, a tradition of declamation in delivery, and many other factors demanded an external--or "technical"--acting style. Voice, breathing, and elocution exercises were compulsory, as was training in dance, mime, acrobatics, juggling, swordplay, posture and balance.

When judging external acting, consider:

- *Voice*: Is the voice musical and pleasant to listen to? Does the actor use a variety of vocal levels, color, volume, and resonance? Can the actor be heard and understood?
- *Physical*: Does the actor move gracefully and with purpose? Are gestures controlled and focused, or random and non-specific? Is the actor at ease? Are there nervous "ticks" or other physical distractions? Is it the "character" or the "actor" who evidences such distractions?

External or technical acting does not preclude strongly felt inner emotion. In ancient Greece, Aristotle told actors, "Those who feel emotion are most convincing through natural sympathy with the characters they represent." Shakespeare counseled actors to "suit the action to the word, the word to the action, with this special observance, that you o'erstep not the modesty of nature."

These comments by Aristotle and Shakespeare point the way towards *internal acting*, largely a modern and Western approach to performance. The discussion plays of Ibsen and the subtle dramas of Anton Chekhov demanded an intimacy in playing style. Internal actors, such as Dustin Hoffman or Meryl Streep, usually tap their inner resources by using *emotion memory*, among other things, to project themselves into the characters they play. Emotion memory asks actors to summon up memories of personal experiences and the attendant emotions that are comparable to those of the scripted characters. Internal actors can place too much emphasis on inner feeling, however, which can lead to self-indulgence (or "private moments") and a breakdown of the vocal and physical demands of performance.

Though it is not necessary to have formal training, a knowledge of fundamental technique can enliven your reading and viewing experiences. Actors must confront three texts:

1. The scripted *text* as written by the playwright (assuming that the play is not improvised);
2. The *context* or situation in which the characters find themselves;
3. The *subtext* (what the text actually implies).

There is also the *intentional purpose* of the text: that is, why the character must say those lines at that point in time. For an instant acting lesson, say the simple line "*Don't go.*" Now repeat the line as if:

- Your lover is about to walk out the door after an argument.
- Your room mate wants to drive to the store in the midst of a terrible storm.
- Your child is trying to sneak off to play with friends before the chores are done.

Without much thought or training you probably came up with a good subtext for each situation. Your subtext (literally, "the text beneath the text") for the first was probably something like, "I love you, don't leave me, I can't live without you!" Perhaps your subtext for the second was "Don't be a fool, you could get killed," while the third was "You're in big trouble!" In each case there was a very specific reason (intention, motivation, goal) for saying the line (i.e. to salvage a love affair, to protect a friend, to admonish a child).

Many actors, acting teachers, and directors prefer the phrase "fight for" instead of intentions and motivations because it imparts the urgency demanded by drama. Directors challenge actors, "What are you fighting for and what will you do to get it?" One of the beauties--and, to be sure, frustrations--of acting is that there are so many possible answers for these questions. This is where actors must finally make "choices" to define their characters' intentions, their obstacles, and especially the strategies they will use to overcome them. When evaluating an actor, consider the variety of tactical and responsive choices he or she makes; if an actor relies too heavily on a single choice (anger, shouting, flailing arms and gestures), it is not likely to be a very memorable—or truthful—performance. Human beings are complex and an actor needs to show that complexity in the number and variety of emotional, physical and vocal choices he or she makes.

Think of an actor as a piano player. How many keys is he or she using in a performance? If only 20 or 30 of the emotional keys are being used out of the possible 88, then it is likely the performance will not be very compelling—nor truthful! You can apply this same analogy to the actor's vocal work (though bland vocal work may be the result of weak, predictable intentional choices).

Today both external and especially internal actors break a script into its smallest parts--the *beat*, a line, or portion of a longer line, in which the character has a specific intention. Each time the intention changes, a new beat begins. Beats evolve into *units* (usually a section of a scene), units become scenes, and scenes become acts, each of which has its dominant intention, the whole of which is defined by an overall intention. You'll find reading and watching a play a richer experience if you become sensitive to these divisions and, more importantly, the intentions and obstacles confronting every character in the play. Every speech in a play is important, if only for a moment.

Whatever their approach to acting, performers are after one thing: a truthful representation of life and its dilemmas, though not necessarily in 'realistic' terms. Remember, however, that terms such as "truthful," "natural," and especially "lifelike" are always relative when applied to acting and must be considered in light of the age in which they are used. Do you, for instance, think that the acting style of a 1920s silent movie is as "natural" as that of a recent film with Tom Hanks or Gwyneth Paltrow?

Most of the discussion thus far has centered on the individual actor, but only in one man or one woman shows does an actor work alone. Thus *ensemble* is also an important term when evaluating the performances in a play. Each of the actors—from the 'stars' to the 'walk-ons'—ought to perform in the same style, at the same level of energy, with the same sense of purpose. Good actors listen to each other, and then build on one another's speeches. Their collective timing is crisp; they are not afraid to cut one another off (if the action requires it); and they create a group dynamic on stage. Though the leading roles may monopolize your attention, one of the best indicators of a quality production is how well the smaller roles are played.

Evaluating the Actors

When you attend a play, you might consider some of the following questions while completing the worksheet on evaluating the performance of the actors. These are offered only as a starting point, and as you spend more evenings in the theater observing actors up close (as opposed to on the movie or TV screen), you will develop additional criteria:

Exterior Technique:
- Is the voice audible? clear? strong? resonant? intelligible? colorful?
- Does the actor's physical presence command attention?
- Does the actor move well?
- Are gestures fluid, natural, and befitting the character?
- Is the actor energetic or lethargic?
- Is the body attitude telling us something about the character? Is it telling us too much; i.e., is the actor "mugging" or "indicating" rather than using other elements to communicate the character's feelings?
- Does the actor stay focused and "in character" or does he or she drop in and out of character?

Interior Technique:
- Are the actor's intentions clear?
- Are the choices (tactics) inventive and fresh, or are they clichéd and predicable?
- Are the choices consistent with the character's psychology? (Or, are they consistently inconsistent when the character is fraught with inconsistencies?)
- Are there a variety of choices, especially emotionally?
- Does the actor resort to a single reaction (e.g., anger)?
- Does the actor support the emotional choices with strong, clear physical actions? (Is the voice telling us one thing while the body tells us another?)

Ensemble:
- Do the actors play to and off one another well?
- Do they listen to each other? Build on one another's reactions?
- Is there a unity of acting style?
- Do the voices match one another?
- Is the pacing and cueing appropriate to the situation?
- Do the actors collectively build and sustain dramatic tension?

Scene 5:
The Designers

The very term *theater*--"the seeing place"--implies that the visual dimension is an important part of the audience's experience. Often our memories of an evening in the theater are most colored by what we have seen. Even the simplest of scenery can delight as much as the spectacular sets of the biggest, splashiest Broadway musical. A single, well-chosen costume piece can say as much about a character as a magnificent dress or a well-tailored suit. Make-up can transform an actor into an extraordinary being. And lighting and sound can create atmosphere and mood instantaneously.

On the other hand splendid costumes and scenery, scintillating lighting or sound effects can also detract from a performance if they dominate the acting and the storytelling. As with all things in theater, balance among its elements is important, and you, as critic, should be aware of the contributions (or liabilities) of the design elements.

The Design Team

In your program you will find a list of artists who comprise the design team, and each is supported by other skilled technicians who help bring the design to its realization. (By the way, that's one reason why tickets to live professional theater are somewhat expensive; there are many highly trained and talented artists supporting the actors.)

A production design team typically consists of:

- *Scene Designer*: who creates the scenery and draws up the blueprints, which are used by various scenic artists, such as:
    o Technical Director, who oversees the building of the scenery
    o Carpenters and assorted specialty craft-persons
    o Scene painters
    o Property Masters
    o Special effects artists

- *Costume Designer*, who creates the costumes and provides instructions to those who create the costumes, such as:
    o A costumier, who supervises the various costume artists
    o Pattern makers

- Cutters and stitchers
- Dyers
- Trim artists
- Wig specialists
- Dressers

- *Make-up Designer*, who creates and then usually teaches the actors to apply makeup for especially complex designs.

- *Lighting Designer*, who devises a "plot" for the lights that indicates position, number, and kind of lighting instruments, gels (colors), gobos (metal discs for patterns) and other filters; the designer is assisted by
  - a *Master Electrician* and an electrical crew;
  - Light board operator(s)

- *Sound Designer*, who helps select the sound (music, special effects, and other ambient sound) and speaker locations for the production. The designer supervises the making of a master tape or CD that can be played by the *sound board operator.*

The Functions of the Designs

Designers in the contemporary theater work closely with the director in developing and realizing the concept for a play. Though each designer has objectives particular to his or her area of expertise, there are some common requirements of scenic, costume, lighting and sound designs:

- They should be consistent within the directorial concept and they should complement each other to re-enforce the production's visual metaphor.
- They support the work of the actors functionally and aesthetically by providing focus upon the actors.
- They help establish the style of production and its degree of reality or theatricality.
- They re-enforce the emotional atmosphere of the production.
- They provide the audience with relevant information about the historical period, the locale, the characters and their relationships with one another and their environment.

To put it succinctly, good designs work together to create exactly the right world for *this* play as interpreted by *this* production.

Design Choices

While actors talk about subtext and motivations to describe their craft, designers refer to line, mass, form, color, palette, silhouette, balance, symmetry, asymmetry, intensity, texture, and much more to define their concerns. Each play will alter the manner in which they are used. For instance, line--e.g., straight, curved, geometric shapes, irregular--might suggest conflict if predominantly curved lines converge on sharp, angular ones. Mass--the comparative size of objects--can suggest oppression. There are silhouettes for comedy (oversized, rounded, horizontal, slightly out-of-balance) just as there are for weightier plays (proportioned, straight lines, vertical). Color and intensity affect moods and perceptions. It is quite possible for designers to create false impressions by using design elements ironically.

Texture can subtly--even subliminally--affect an audience's perception of the play. Rough textures, such as coarse or brocaded cloth, pocked stones, weathered wood, decaying metalwork, can add weight to a serious play. Lighting designers prefer heavily textured sets and costumes because they produce interesting effects by creating sharper contrasts between light and shadow. A comedic play may benefit from smoother textures; in a comedy colorfully dressed characters can leap out from surfaces with flatter textures, especially when brightly lit.

Set designers know that scenery must be more than a mere backdrop for the action. Because the audience often sees the scenery before the play begins, the scene design may be the first element to affect their response to a play. And just as the playwright must create intrigue for the audience by the way the play is structured, so, too, must the scene designer arouse the audience's "expectancy" when it first looks at the setting. An aptly chosen metaphor or symbol may suggest the thematic concerns of the play. The Guthrie Theatre's 1985 production of *A Midsummer Night's Dream* featured an enormous moon as its primary set piece; it seemed to say "moonstruck" people do bizarre things.

The scene designer's first task, however, is to transform a bare space into an environment for the actors to do their work. Though the design should have an aesthetic appeal, it needs to be practical by providing entrances and exits, playing levels that encourage a variety of stage pictures, and places to sit, stand, or recline. The space must also encourage actors to move in other than straight lines--yet the set cannot become an obstacle course. Furthermore, a good set design provides focal points for key moments of action; down stage center may be a traditional "hot spot" on stage, but designers seek alternatives. While the scenery must support the actors' work, it cannot dominate them--even in plays where the environment overwhelms the characters. If the audience is distracted by an overly massive or too cluttered scenic environment, it tends to stop listening and merely looks at the setting.

A word about realistic settings may be useful. Given a choice, it is safe to say most scene designers in the contemporary theater would avoid completely realistic settings, partly because it reduces their task to mere reproduction, but primarily because they have learned that there are more interesting alternatives. Thus, realistic settings can run the gamut from ultra-realism (sometimes called "kitchen-sink realism") to "impressionistic" scenery in which the designer merely suggests reality by very selectively choosing only those elements absolutely necessary to suggest locale: partial walls, doors suspended in space, skeletal outlines of architectural features. Can an essentially realistic play be performed in a realistic acting style on a less-than-realistic set? Yes, and in some ways the performances gain from the apparent contradiction in styles. Premium emphasis is placed on the actors and the audience can focus on their interactions rather than on the clutter of the kitchen behind them.

Costume designers also have their particular concerns. "Dressing" the actors is complicated by the fact that stage clothing--even in realistic plays--is not the same thing as everyday apparel. While what we choose to wear as we dress in the morning helps define our personalities to some extent, costumes in a play have to tell us much more about the characters. Shakespeare's observation that "the apparel oft proclaims the man" is particularly true of stage costumes. A thoughtfully conceived costume is among the most expedient ways to define a character, almost instantaneously.

Not only do costumes tell us much about the individual characters, they show relationships among the characters. Major characters are distinguished from minor ones, and groups are contrasted with one another through a costume plot, a term that suggests that the designer must calculate effects as carefully as the playwright plots the story.

Much of the lighting designer's work is mechanical and is undertaken solely to make sure the actors are visible. The artistic dimension involves planning intensities, back and side lighting, fade times, and so on. Much of this work can only be done in final rehearsals when the other components are brought together. A good lighting plot is the glue that binds all of the visual resources that go into a play.

Sound cues must also be meticulously planned and rehearsed. At technical rehearsals, much time is spent finding the right volume levels, placement of sound, and fade times. Not only do sound designers create the auditory support for a play, they also develop microphone systems to insure that actors can be heard, especially in musicals and in large outdoor theaters that are central to the summer festival phenomenon.

The award-winning costume designer Theoni V. Aldredge argues that "good design is design you are not aware of." Strange talk from an artist in such a visual medium as costume design! She means that a good design does not compete with a production, but enhances it.

Evaluating the Designs

You might determine how well the design elements enhance a performance by considering some of the following questions as you complete the *Evaluating the Designs* worksheet on page 58 of the appendix:

- Are the various design elements unified? Do they complement or compete with one another?
- Is there a discernable pattern that unites the designs?
- Is there sufficient variety and contrast within the unified concept to add interest?
- Do the design elements help the audience distinguish major, secondary, and minor characters?
- Do the design elements provide focus where it should be placed?
- Do the design elements allow the actors to be clearly seen? Heard? Move freely?
- Do the design elements create a coherent world for the production?
- Do they provide sufficient information that helps define time, place, and character?

- Are any of the designs "too busy" (i.e., do they distract rather than provide focus)?
- Is there an intellectual foundation to the designs--such as an apt metaphor?
- Do the design elements--individually and collectively--add to the aesthetic enjoyment of the production?

NOTES

ACT THREE:
WRITING THE REVIEW

The Post Mortem

After a production has closed, many professional theater companies hold a "post mortem" (literally, "after the death") in which the production team discusses those elements that worked well in a production and those that perhaps didn't work. This is theater's version of "quality control" and the artists—who are quite used to criticism—use the post mortem to get constructive feedback from their colleagues. Also, if there were communication breakdowns or other technical difficulties, the post mortem provides a good opportunity to devise solutions so that similar problems will not recur.

The review you will write allows you to perform a post mortem on the production, to evaluate its strengths and weaknesses. You may not be able to influence future productions, but you will enhance your own critical thinking skills.

Scene 1
The Production Review

Typically, a production review is a relatively short response to the play and its performance, and it is written shortly after the critic has seen the production. (Professional critics often have less than an hour to write their reviews!) Usually, the reviewer does not go back for a second look--though one of the advantages of a college production is that it is accessible and usually inexpensive. It may be possible (and useful) to see a show twice if circumstances permit.

The production review customarily assesses two things:
1. *The play itself* (i.e. the script written by the playwright, assuming the production is not improvised);
2. *The production* of the play (i.e., the acting, the direction, the designs, and the technical support).

By the conclusion of your review, the reader ought to have a good idea of what the play is about, what it says, how well it says it, and the quality of its realization in live performance. It is quite possible you may admire the play but have reservations about the performance--or vice versa. You may like elements of the plot or character, but have questions about other aspects of the scripted play, just as you may find some actors quite good, others less so.

A good review is:

- *Balanced*: it neither uniformly praises a play and its production, nor does it unrelentingly castigate both. There are certainly times when a play gets a thoroughly glowing review, just as there are times when a thundering pan (i.e., negative review) is given. In most cases you will find that even the best plays and productions could be improved upon, while even the weakest at least show some potential. Good reviewers are sensitive to both possibilities.

- *Vivid and specific* because they go a long way toward recreating the theater event for the reader who ought to be able to visualize some elements of the production.

Scene 2:
Preparing to Write the Review

Although you may have read the play before you saw it, a second reading (if possible) may help jar your memory after you've seen it. Jot down your ideas, key points, memorable lines and stage moments as you reread the text. If you don't have access to the script, mentally "replay" the production. Those lines or moments you remember most vividly (especially the next day) are probably your best source of inspiration as you prepare to write.

Perhaps you took some notes during the production (remember: unobtrusively!). Review these and try to recreate the moment you've noted in your mind's eye. Also, review the program, especially the director's note and other supplemental material. You may find ideas and perhaps even quotations you can use here. If you discussed the play with someone who attended the theater with you, recall the things that were said, particularly comments that were made most enthusiastically—or otherwise.

Once you've relived the production and collected some notes, organize your ideas into a rough outline, using the suggestions for organization described in the following section titled *Shaping the Review*. Like a good play, a review also has an intriguing beginning, a well-developed middle, and a memorable ending.

Scene 3:
Shaping the Review

Setting the Stage: Your Introduction

A well-written review begins with a "grabber," a vivid introduction that tells the reader something about the play, the production, and the reviewer's overall opinion of the event. It also prompts the reader to continue. In short, a review opens much like a good play in production: it draws the audience into the play, raises questions about the experience to come, and establishes a dominant idea to be explored. Here is a fine example taken from a review of August Wilson's *Ma Rainey's Black Bottom*, it was written by Frank Rich of the *New York Times* (1984):

> Late in Act I of *Ma Rainey's Black Bottom*, a somber, aging
> band trombonist (Joe Seneca) tilts his head heavenward to sing
> the blues. The setting is a dilapidated Chicago recording studio
> of 1927, and the song sounds as old as time. "If I had my way,"
> goes the lyric, "I would tear this building down." Once the play has
> ended that lyric has almost become a prophecy. In *Ma Rainey's
> Black Bottom*, the writer August Wilson sends the entire history of
> black America crashing down upon our heads. The play is a
> searing inside account of what white racism does to its victims--
> and it floats on the same authentic artistry as the blues music it
> celebrates.

Note how this introduction captures some of the energy of the performance, as well as satisfying the reader's need to know what the play is about and whether it is a worthwhile experience.

Summarizing the Play

Having secured the reader's interest, the reviewer then moves on to a summary of the play's plot and its thematic intentions. Plot summaries should be brief, usually no more than two to three sentences. Identify the principal characters and the conflicts in which they are engaged. It is not the reviewer's job to reveal how the conflicts are resolved--unless, of course, the playwright has contrived the resolution implausibly. While summarizing the plot the reviewer should also indicate something about the ambience of the work. This is especially important when environment is important to the play or when directors and designers have placed the setting in another milieu.

The Playwright's Intentions and/or the Directorial Concept

After identifying the play's issues (e.g., a dejected salesman can no longer "cut it" on the road), the reviewer comments on its thematic values. Even the frothiest musical, such as *Forty-Second Street*, offers a simple idea ("perseverance and a little bit of luck ultimately pays off"). Great plays, those that we call "universal," usually suggest a number of themes. And it is entirely possible, even probable, that a production will explore one of those themes in a new or controversial manner, as when Baz Luhrman reset Shakespeare's *Romeo and Juliet* in a vaguely Miami Beach milieu for his 1996 film. Often the most interesting conflict in a production is the one between the playwright and director, and the reviewer needs to address this issue. Reviewers ought to be confident enough to suggest an interpretation of the play (readers know it is not necessarily definitive). Such analyses are most credible when they are supported with specific evidence such as lines from the text or the recreation of a particular moment that illustrates the theme. Comments about the originality or profundity of the play's themes are a useful way to conclude the discussion of the script.

The Performers

A significant portion of the review must evaluate the performances of the principal actors, and perhaps lesser ones whose work is especially noteworthy. While it is easy to toss around well-worn adjectives to describe actors--"scintillating," "memorable," "convincing," or "poor"--it is more useful (and challenging) to describe the actor at work. Rich's comments on Theresa Merritt's performance as Ma Rainey accomplish this:

> [She] is Ma Rainey incarnate. A singing actress of both wit and power, she finds bitter humor in the character's distorted sense of self: When she barks her outrageous demands to [the black musicians], we see a show business monster who's come a long way from her roots. Yet the roots can still be unearthed. In a rare reflective moment, she explains why she sings the blues. "You

don't sing to feel better," Miss Merritt says tenderly. "You sing because that's a way of understanding life."

Here we get both a sense of the actor's emotional range and the reality of the character she creates. Never do we doubt that Miss Merritt was "scintillating" or "memorable;" but here we understand why Rich judged her performance positively.

A note about negative criticism is in order because some reviewers often use it as an opportunity to show off their own wit rather than to remedy a weak performance. Even good reviewers succumb to this temptation, as when John Mason Brown dismissed Tallulah Bankhead's performance in Shakespeare's *Antony and Cleopatra:* "[She] barged down the Nile as Cleopatra last night--and sank." It is more constructive to discuss an actor's lack of emotional range or predictable vocal patterns than to summarize his or her work as "poor" or "uninteresting." Though it is unlikely actors will read your reviews, discussing acting strengths and weaknesses in concrete terms is a constructive way for you to hone your critical thinking skills.

You may not have space or time to assess every actor's performance, but often you can single out a minor role and comment on the artistry an actor brings to it. And by all means, be sure to assess the ensemble effect of a production. A play dominated by a single actor may not, in the end, be as satisfying as one in which all actors--from stars to spear carriers--are contributing equally to the quality of the performance.

The Design Elements

Designers do not want to read that their sets, costumes, and lighting were little more than "beautiful," "electric," or "marvelous." They want to know that their artistry contributed to the mood and ambience of the play--and perhaps even its thematic intentions. Judge the design and technical work within the context of the whole production and not merely as a visual delight. Jo Mielziner's design for the 1949 Broadway production of *Death of a Salesman* was thoughtfully crystallized by T. C. Worsley in *The New Statesman* (August 6, 1949): "The stage design is skeletal; we see all three rooms at once, and we see, even more important, looming up behind, the great lowering claustrophobic cliff of concrete skyscraper in which their living space is embedded." Writing like this elevates reviewing to an art form.

You may discuss the designs in any order you wish, though it may be best to begin with the most striking design elements. And you need not go into detail about every design element; there may be some plays in which costumes are not as important as other elements. Most professional reviews—for better or worse—rarely devote more than a single paragraph to the designs, unless the designs are the dominant feature of the production.

Bringing Down the Curtain: Your Conclusion

Your review ought to close with a brief statement that not only summarizes the impact the production you saw, but that also beckons the reader to share in the experience. Rich's review of *Ma Rainey's Black Bottom* accomplishes this:

> The lines [see comments on Merritt's acting above] might also apply to the play's author. Mr. Wilson can't mend the broken lives he unravels in *Ma Rainey's Black Bottom*. But, like his heroine, he makes their suffering into art that forces us to understand and won't allow us to forget.

Finally, it might be useful to hear the words of a theater artist about the role of the critic-reviewer in the theater. Jack O'Brien is the artistic director of the Globe Theatre in San Diego and a successful Broadway director of such plays as *The Full Monty*:

> Years ago I used to love the early reviews of Walter Kerr, and I used to hold them up to our critics today--and still do--because to write great criticism, to read criticism is not to hear something brilliantly torn apart and dissected and dismissed. It's to make you or somebody get off their dead asses and go out and buy a ticket. And if you can do that, I think you belong in some proximity to the theater. Not just to say, "This is what it means" and "This is where it's deficient," but to say, "If you care, see that performance. This actor is not delivering yet, but you're watching somebody beginning to achieve greatness." Or to create the idea that it *might* happen.

Scene 4:
Some Technical Matters

Quotations and Citations

Writing about drama raises particular problems, especially where quotations are concerned. Because you will be using a number of quotations, it is cumbersome and distracting to use footnotes after every quotation. After an initial foot or endnote, you can usually identify the quote in parentheses, using one of several systems. In general, quotations of one-act verse dramas, such as Greek tragedies, are identified by line numbers, which are usually placed along the right hand margin of the script (this may vary with publishers). Most classical dramas, such as those of Shakespeare and his contemporaries, use act, scene, and line number(s) to identify quotations. You might see Hamlet's "To be or not to be" identified as III.1.55-ff. which means it is found in act three, scene one, line 55 and following (or lines 55-89 if the full speech is cited). If you are dealing with several plays and have not specifically identified a quotation by play in your text, use a standard abbreviation for the play prior to the line numbers (e.g., *Hamlet* is *Ham.*, while *A Midsummer Night's Dream* is usually *MND*). Quotations from most modern plays are usually identified by the page number of the script from which they are taken. In all cases, however, you need to cite the specific text from which you have quoted the lines; this is especially important for some classic plays because lines may actually be numbered differently from text to text.

There are two ways to cite the text (you can use a footnote for the first quotation). Your instructor will probably indicate which method is preferred:

1. Provide all of the bibliographic information and add a phrase such as "all quotations are to this text and will hereafter be cited parenthetically;
2. List the text in a "Works Cited" appendage at the end of the paper.

Lengthy quotations from plays (that is, those over three lines long) should be set off from your text; this is usually done by indenting five spaces and single-spacing the quotation. If it is written in verse, it should be reproduced as verse in your paper. You should make every effort to reproduce the verse as it is laid out in the original text by indenting appropriate lines. The shared line of Elizabethan playwriting would look like this:

QUEEN: Why, how now, Hamlet?
HAMLET: What's the matter now?
QUEEN: Have you forgot me?
HAMLET: No, by the rood, not so.

(*H.*, III.4. 13-14)

Note that long quotations do not require quotation marks as they are clearly separated from your writing. Shorter quotes can be incorporated into the regular text by placing them in quotation marks. Any parentheses with line or page numbers are placed outside the quotation marks. If you are quoting a couple of lines of verse, you should indicate where the break in the verse line is by using a slash mark and capitalizing the second line. Thus, Hamlet's question "What is a man,/If his chief good and market of his time/Be but to sleep and feed?" (IV.4.33-35) should be typed as you read it here. (*Note*: the "I" in "If" is capitalized because it is capitalized in the text; if it is not capitalized, you do not capitalize it. If you wish to indicate it as a lower case "t" because it is in the middle of your sentence, you would bracket your alteration from the original: "[I]f the chief good...")

Titles

Titles of full-length plays are customarily identified by underlining or italicizing them (though newspapers generally put titles of plays in quotation marks); short plays (one acts) are designated by quotation marks. This system usually allows the reader to tell the length of an unfamiliar play without further identification. If your instructor has not indicated a specific format for annotations and bibliography (such as the *MLA* or *Chicago Manual of Style*), use one with which you are familiar or invest in a guidebook. The important thing is to be consistent in whichever format you use.

EVALUATING A PERFORMANCE

Play: _____

Playwright: _____   Date of Composition: _____

Country of Origin: _____   Style/Genre: _____

Source(s) (if known):

CHARACTERS: Identify and briefly describe the characters:
   Protagonist(s):

   Antagonist(s):

   Secondary Characters:

CONFLICT: What is the primary external and internal conflict to be resolved by the central character?

   External:

   Internal:

PLOT:
Plot Type (circle one): LINEAR   EPIC   CYCLIC   PLOTLESS

Summarize the plot in 2-3 sentences:

Summarize the subplot(s) in 1 sentence (when applicable) and indicate how the subplot(s) illuminate the main plot?

THEME: Define the theme/message in a sentence; use a quote from the play if appropriate:

STYLISTIC FEATURES: Discuss the distinctive features of the play that help define its style, acting and production challenges, etc. Why is the play representative of its style/genre/country of origin?

THEATRICALITY: What makes this play "good theater?"

DRAMATIC APPEAL: What makes this play "good drama?"

REPRESENTATIVE QUOTE: Copy (or paraphrase) a significant line or speech from the play and explain its importance:

Terminology for Evaluating a Performance Worksheet

DATE OF COMPOSITION: What year was the play written?

COUNTRY OF ORIGIN: In what country was the play written and/or first produced?

SOURCES: As you read about the play, perhaps you will discover something about how the playwright was inspired to write the play. Perhaps it is based on an earlier work, an incident in the playwright's life, or a topical event. Such information can be useful and interesting both as you read the play and as you write the review. Briefly note any sources of inspiration here.

GENRE: What is the literary classification of the play? Tragedy? Comedy? Tragicomedy? Or one of the subsets of these principal genres. *See p. 8 for a list of genres*; refer to appropriate sections in your textbook or its glossary if you need help defining these terms.

STYLE: What is the primary performance mode? Realistic? Classical? Expressionistic? Absurdist? There are many styles, and they are not always easy to pin down. As you read about the play, you will very likely find some reference to its style.

PLOT: Circle the plot type:

    1. **The climactic plot**: The most traditional form of plotting, the climactic (or linear) plot begins with the exposition of a problem, builds on a series of minor crises to a major climax and its resolution. Causality is paramount in climactic plotting; that is, one event precipitates another. It is possible to have several linear plots (or subplots).

    2. **The episodic (epic) plot**: consists of a series events, often taking place over a period of time and in many locales, that are related thematically if not always by a single dramatic action. Most novels and the great myths such as *The Iliad* are episodic, as are Shakespeare's history plays.

    3. **The cyclic plot**: some dramas employ the cyclic plot that, intentionally, does not achieve a resolution, but instead end much the way they began to suggest the futility of human action.

    4. **The "plotless" play**: Many recent Western plays adhere to the theory that conventional artistic forms (e.g. the traditional plot) no longer reflect the reality of human experience.

CHARACTERS: Identify only the most important characters. Usually there is only a single protagonist or antagonist, but there may be more than one (e.g., Romeo and Juliet). Be especially attentive to "archetypal" and "stock" characters. As you read and see more plays, you will more easily recognize character types. List only the 2-3 most important secondary characters.

STYLISTIC FEATURES: This includes such things as poetry, music, dance, masks, mime, asides, soliloquies, 'freezes,' etc. If the play is 'realistic,' its stylistic features are less apparent because what you see and hear is intended to look like 'real life' on stage. The most obvious stylistic features are those that are more theatrical than realistic.

THEATRICALITY: Discuss why the play is "good theater," i.e., those visual, aural, or staging elements that contribute to the entertainment and aesthetic experience. These may not be readily apparent in a reading, so it is important that you try to "see" and "hear" the play as you read it. Obviously, you could write a whole paper about this topic; concentrate on 1-2 examples of exceptional theatricality.

DRAMATIC APPEAL: This refers to the literary elements such as plot, conflict, structure, language, etc. Keep in mind that tastes in dramatic literature may vary from one culture to another. Something which our high-energy, action-oriented culture may find "boring," may be extraordinary to another culture that prizes contemplative, quiet drama (e.g., Japanese Noh drama). Approach each play with an open mind, much as you would if you were visiting a foreign country.

REPRESENTATIVE QUOTE: Select a short passage/speech/line that you find especially appealing, memorable, etc. If it is lengthy, you may identify it by a short section or phrase. In a sentence, explain why the passage appeals to you.

Appendix B:
Evaluating the Director

Name of Play/Production: _____

Production Company: _____

Name of Theater: _____ Dates of Production: _____

Name of Director: _____

List 3-4 of the director's most important previous productions (see program):

Interpretation/Concept:
Is there a logical, coherent interpretation of the play?   YES   NO
- In 1-2 sentences summarize what you perceive to be the directorial concept?

Does the script support this interpretation/concept?   YES   NO
- If the director has chosen to play against the script, is there a logic to the alternative interpretation?   Identify the success or weakness of the interpretation.

Does the director seem to dominate the script?   YES   NO
- Explain why you believe the director dominates the script:

Is the storyline clear and comprehensible, and are key moments of exposition, crisis, climax, and resolution marked?   YES   NO
- Discuss any particular strengths and/or weaknesses in the story-telling, noting whether the storytelling is the playwright's or the director's weakness:

Visual Elements
Is there a variety of pleasing stage pictures?   YES   NO
- Describe at least one stage picture that you believed to be especially powerful:

Are entrances/exits well planned, especially crowd scenes (if any)?   YES   NO
- Describe an especially strong and/or weak entrance/exit:

Are actors grouped so that proper focus is given to key characters?   YES   NO
- Describe an especially effective and/or weak example of focus:

Are the theatrical elements coordinated to produce a unified effect?   YES   NO
- Explain any perceived lack of unity in the designs or technical elements:

Aesthetics:
Does the play flow smoothly from one scene to the next?   YES   NO
Does the production have effective rhythm and tempo?   YES   NO
Is there sufficient variety in the pace of the play?   YES   NO
- Identify any weaknesses in pacing and tempo:

Do the various aesthetic elements call attention to themselves or are they integrated into the whole?   DISTRACTING   INTEGRATED
- Discuss any especially distracting elements:

Ensemble:
Has the director created an ensemble among the actors?   YES   NO
Are the acting styles compatible?   YES   NO
Do the actors--individually and collectively--have a well-defined sense of the play's intellectual and emotional intentions?   YES   NO
- Discuss any particular strengths and /or weaknesses in the ensemble:

Evaluating the Acting

Name of Play/Production: _____

Production Company: _____

Names of Principal Actors and Character(s) Played:
ACTOR   CHARACTER(S):

Names of Supporting Actors and Character(s) Played:
ACTOR   CHARACTER(S):

Name of especially noteworthy small role actor/character(s) played:

NOTE: Because there may be many actors in a production, you cannot do a worksheet for each principal and secondary actor. Use this worksheet to assess the work of the most noteworthy actors—i.e. strongest and weakest—using some of the following criteria:

Exterior Technique:
- Is the voice audible? clear? strong? resonant? intelligible? colorful?
Comment on the vocal work of the actor(s); cite specific examples:

- Does the actor's physical presence command attention? Does the actor move well? Are gestures fluid, natural, and befitting the character?
Comment on the physical work of the actors; cite specific examples:

- Is the actor energetic or lethargic?

Comment on the energy level of the actors:

- Does the actor stay focused and "in character" or does he or she drop in and out of character? Comments and examples:

Interior Technique:
- Are the actor's intentions clear? Comments:

- Are the choices (tactics) inventive and fresh, or are they clichéd and predicable? Are the choices consistent with the character's psychology? Comments:

- Are there a variety of choices, especially emotionally? Does the actor resort to a single reaction (e.g., anger)? Does the actor support the emotional choices with strong, clear physical actions? (Is the voice telling us one thing, while the body tells us another?) Comments:

Ensemble:
- Do the actors play to and off one another well? Do they listen to each other? Build on one another's reactions? Comments and examples of ensemble work:

- Is there a unity of acting style? Cite an actor who seemed out of synch with the others:

- Is the pacing and cueing appropriate to the situation? Do the actors collectively build and sustain dramatic tension? Comments with examples of strong/weak pacing and tension:

In your estimation, who was the strongest actor in the cast? Explain your choice:

The weakest? Explain your choice:

Describe the most memorable moment of acting in the production:

Appendix D:
Evaluating the Designs

Name of Play/Production: _____

Production Company: _____

Names of the Design Team:

    Scene Designer: _____

    Costume Designer": _____

    Make-up Designer: _____

    Lighting Designer: _____

    Sound Designer: _____

Unity and Concept:
- Is there an intellectual foundation to the designs--such as an apt metaphor? YES NO

Describe the central design concept/metaphor and cite examples especially effective design choices; be sure to note evidence in the text that supports the design choices:

- Are the various design elements unified? YES NO

Discuss those elements that unify the design, OR any perceived lack of unity in the designs:

- Is there sufficient variety and contrast within the concept to add interest? YES NO

Describe an especially effective use of variety and/or contrast in the designs:

Ambience:
- Do the design elements create a coherent world for the production? YES NO
- Would you characterize the designs as REALISTIC or THEATRICAL? In what 'style' would you label the designs (e.g. 'selective realism,' 'expressionistic,' or...)? Explain the reason for your characterization:

- Do the designs provide information that define time, place, and character? YES NO

Discuss the effectiveness of the ability of the designs to create a visually interesting world for this play:

Focus:
- Do the design elements help the audience distinguish major, secondary, and minor characters? YES NO Do the design elements provide focus where it should be placed? YES NO

Describe especially effective design choices that help focus the actors or that diminish focus on the actors:

- Do the design elements allow the actors to be clearly seen? heard? move freely? YES NO

Discuss moments when the designs seemed to inhibit the actors (if any):

Aesthetics:
- Do the design elements--individually and collectively--add to the aesthetic enjoyment of the production?   YES   NO

Discuss the strengths and/or weaknesses of the aesthetic qualities of the designs:

Describe and briefly discuss the most memorable design choices for:

Scenery:

Costumes and Makeup:

Lighting:

Sound (if applicable):

Special effects (if applicable):

Checklist
Evaluating Your Review

(Before you submit your review, use this checklist to evaluate your own work.)

Content:

.   Does the introduction attract the reader's attention with a lively opening that suggests something about the quality of the production?

H   Do the introductory paragraphs clearly indicate the name of the play, the playwright, and the production company?

K   Is the plot summarized briefly and efficiently, without giving away the resolution of the play?

F   Have you identified and discussed the theme(s) of the play?

G   Have you identified the director and discussed what you perceive to be the directorial concept? If there seems to be a discrepancy between the play text and the directorial concept have you addressed this issue?

G   Have you assessed the artistic contributions, including strengths and weaknesses, of: *(select the most applicable artists for this production)*:

       D   Director?
       F   Dance/fight choreographers?
       D   Principal actors?
       D   Noteworthy supporting actors?
       D   Scene designer?
       F   Costume designer?
       G   Make up artist
       d   Special effects artists (if applicable)?
       D   Lighting designer?
       D   Sound designer

D   Have you supported your comments about the script and its themes, the directorial concept, and the specific contributions of the artists with specific examples from the production?

F   Have you noted the audience's response to the play?

G   Have you concluded your review with a memorable statement that invites the reader to see (or avoid) the production?

Style

D   Is the writing lively and filled with descriptive examples that help the reader visualize the production?

F   Is your writing free from clichés and trite critical expressions?[2]

F   Did you carefully proofread your review (preferably out loud) to check for clarity, syntax, and sentence construction?

Format

B   Is the paper properly formatted?
         A Margins?   L Type size?   G Spacing

F   Are titles and foreign words/phrases placed in italics or quotations marks (as per your instructor's instructions)?

F   Are quotations from the play properly indicated, including citations if necessary?

G   Have you checked the spelling of all words, especially the names of the artists and the characters in the play? (Use your program as a guide.)

K   Other items requested by your instructor?

G   Did you give yourself a pat on the back for writing a good review?

---

[2] E.g., "Awesome," "incredible," "wonderful," "boring," "on the edge of your seat," "set your toes to tapping," or "two thumbs up."

NOTES

NOTES

NOTES

NOTES

NOTES

NOTES